JOHN STAINER

The Crucifixion

A MEDITATION ON THE
SACRED PASSION OF THE HOLY REDEEMER

arranged for tenor (or soprano) & bass (or alto) soli,
SSA & organ, with hymns for congregational participation

by Desmond Ratcliffe
Words selected & written by the Reverend J. Sparrow-Simpson, MA

words edition available

NOVELLO

The organ part has been edited by the arranger.

DURATION ABOUT 50 MINUTES

THE CRUCIFIXION

Arranged by
DESMOND RATCLIFFE

JOHN STAINER

1 And they came to a place named Gethsemane

2 The Agony

3

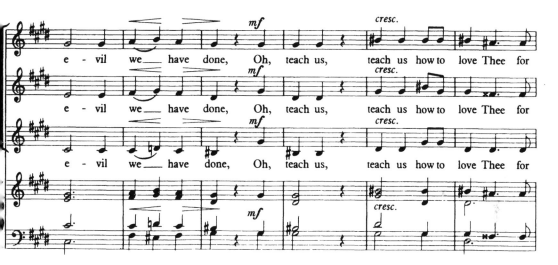

BASS SOLO
or **ALTO SOLO**

Could ye not watch with Me one brief hour? Did ye not say up-on

Ked - ron's slope, Ye would not fall in - to the Temp - ter's

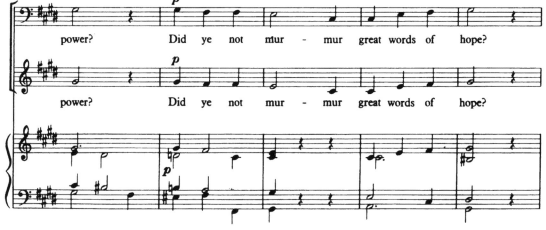

power? Did ye not mur - mur great words of hope?

5

S I FULL
S II Je-su, Lord Je-su, bowed in bit-ter an-guish, and bear-ing all the
A Je-su, Lord Je-su, bowed in bit-ter an-guish, and bear-ing all the
Je-su, Lord Je-su, bowed in bit-ter an-guish, and bear-ing all the

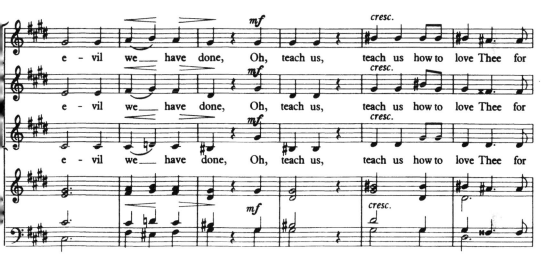

e-vil we__ have done, Oh, teach us, teach us how to love Thee for
e-vil we__ have done, Oh, teach us, teach us how to love Thee for
e-vil we__ have done, Oh, teach us, teach us how to love Thee for

Thy love, Help us to pray, and watch, and mourn__ with Thee.
Thy love, Help us to pray, and watch, and mourn with Thee.
Thy love, Help us to pray, and watch, and mourn with Thee.

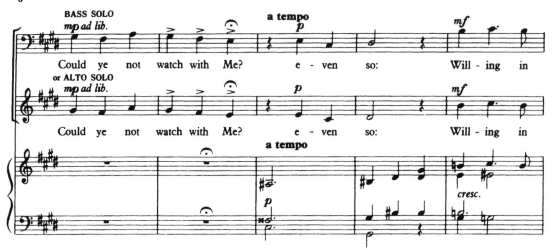

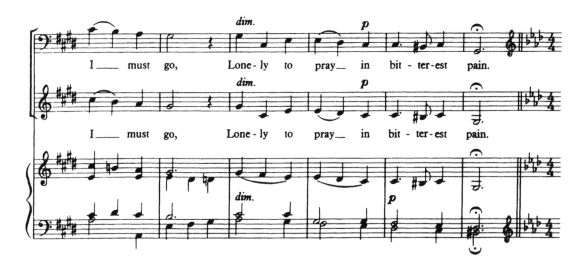

Allegro ♩ = 120

Full Sw.

Man.

TENOR or SOPRANO SOLO

And they laid their hands on Him, and

ad lib.

took Him, and led Him a-way to the high priest.

cresc.

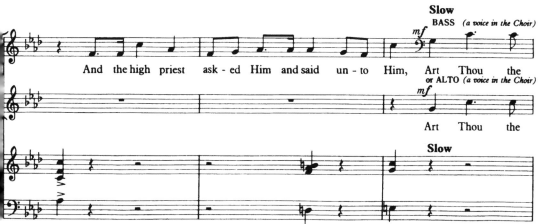

Slow

BASS *(a voice in the Choir)*

And the high priest ask - ed Him and said un - to Him, Art Thou the

or ALTO *(a voice in the Choir)*

Art Thou the

Slow

Christ, the Son of the Bless-ed? Je-sus said, I am: and ye shall

Christ, the Son of the Bless-ed? I am: and ye shall

see the Son of man sit-ting on the right hand of power, and

see the Son of man sit-ting on the right hand of power, and

com-ing in the clouds of heaven. Then the high priest

com-ing in the clouds of heaven.

rent_____ his clothes, and saith: What need

we a - ny fur-ther wit-ness-es? Ye have heard the blas-phe-my. And they all con -

we a - ny fur-ther wit-ness es? Ye have heard the blas-phe-my.

demned Him to be guilt - y of death. And they bound

adagio *cresc.*

Je - sus and car - ried Him a - way, and de - liv - ered Him to Pi - late. And

RECIT. **moderato** *dim.* *p* **a tempo**

Pi - late will - ing to con - tent the peo - ple, re - leas - ed Bar - ab - bas un - to

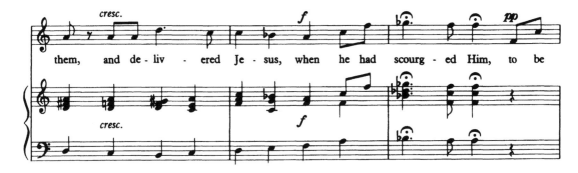

cresc. *f* *pp*

them, and de - liv - ered Je - sus, when he had scourg - ed Him, to be

(pp)

cru - ci - fied. And the sol - diers led Him a - way.

Ped.

attacca

3 Processional to Calvary

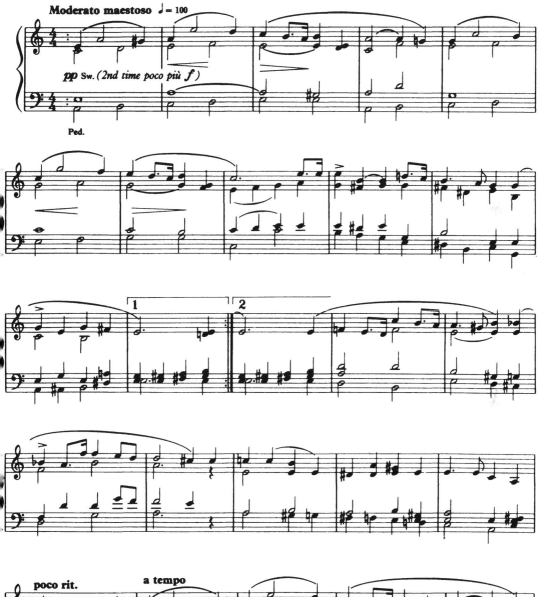

16

poco rit.

a tempo

Solo

p Sw.

Ped.

TENOR or SOPRANO SOLO
p

How sweet is the grace of His

sa - cred Face, And love - ly be -

yond com - pare;

colla voce

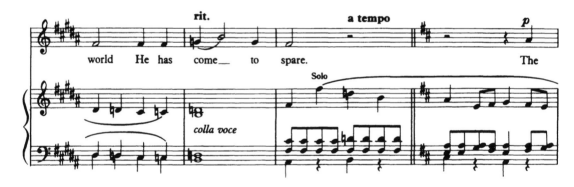

21

on to the end, my God and my Friend, To suf-fer, en-dure and die,_____ to

on to the end, my God and my Friend, To suf-fer, en-dure and die,_____ to

on to the end, my God and my Friend, To suf-fer, en-dure and die,_____ to

suf - fer, en - dure and die.

suf - fer, en - dure and die.

suf - fer, en - dure and die.

16' only

4 And when they had come

attacca

5 The mystery of the divine humiliation

To be sung by the Choir and Congregation

Cross of Je - sus, Cross of Sor-row, Where the Blood of Christ was shed, —

Cross of Je - sus, Cross of__ Sor-row, Where the Blood of__ Christ was shed, —

Cross of Je - sus, Cross of__ Sor-row, Where the Blood of Christ was shed,

Per - fect man on thee was tor-tured, Per - fect God on thee has bled.

Per - fect man on__ thee was tor-tured, Per - fect_God on__ thee has_bled.

Per - fect_man on thee was_ tor-tured, Per - fect_God on__ thee has bled.

Here the King of all the ages,
  Throned in light ere worlds could be
Robed in mortal flesh is dying,
  Crucified by sin for me.

O mysterious condescending!
  O abandonment sublime!
Very God Himself is bearing
  All the sufferings of time!

Evermore for human failure
  By His Passion we can plead;
God has borne all mortal anguish,
  Surely He will know our need.

This—all human thought surpassing—
  This is earth's most awful hour,
God has taken mortal weakness!
  God has laid aside His power!

Once the Lord of brilliant seraphs,
  Winged with Love to do His Will,
Now the scorn of all His creatures,
  And the aim of every ill.

Up in Heaven, sublimest glory
  Circled round Him from the first;
But the earth finds none to serve Him,
  None to quench His raging thirst.

Who shall fathom that descending,
  From the rainbow-circled throne,
Down to earth's most base profaning,
  Dying desolate alone.

From the 'Holy, Holy, Holy,
  We adore Thee, O most High,'
Down to earth's blaspheming voices
  And the shout of 'Crucify.'

Cross of Jesus, Cross of Sorrow,
  Where the Blood of Christ was shed,
Perfect man on thee was tortured,
  Perfect God on thee has bled.

6 He made Himself of no reputation

7 The majesty of the divine humiliation

Moderato ♩ = 100

TENOR or SOPRANO SOLO

King ev-er glo-rious, King ev-er glo-rious! The dews of

death are ga-th'ring round Thee; Up-on the Cross Thy foes have bound Thee— Thy

strength is gone, Thy strength is gone. Not in Thy

Ma — jes-ty, Robed in Heaven's su-prem-est splen-dour, But in weak-ness and sur-

ren - der, Thou hang - est here.

Who can be like Thee? Pi-late high in Zi-on

dwell - ing, Rome with arms the world com - pel - ling, Proud though they be?

Thou art sub - lime, _ Thou art sub - lime: _ Far more

aw - ful in Thy weak - ness, More than king - ly in Thy meek - ness, Thou

32

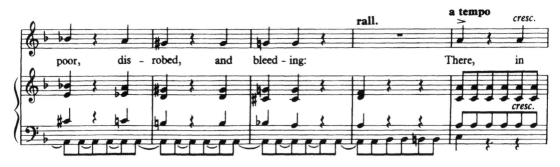

glo – ry in-ter-ced – ing, Thou art the King, Thou art the King!

There, in glo-ry in-ter-ced – ing, there, in glo-ry in-ter-ced – ing, Thou art the

King, Thou art the King, Thou art the King!

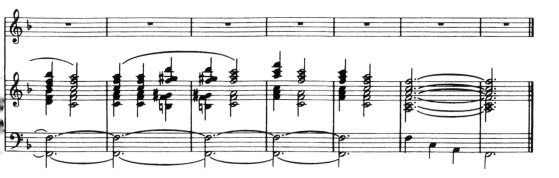

8 And as Moses lifted up the serpent

attacca

9 God so loved the world

liev - eth in Him should not per - ish, should not per - ish, but

liev - eth in Him should not per - ish, should not per - ish, but

liev - eth in Him should not per - ish, should not per - ish, but

have ev - er - last - ing life. For God sent not His Son in - to the

have ev - er - last - ing life. For God sent not His Son in - to the

have ev - er - last - ing life. For God sent not His Son in - to the

world to con - demn the world, God sent not His Son in - to the world to con -

world to con - demn the world, God sent not His Son in - to the world to con -

world to con - demn the world, God sent not His Son in - to the world to con -

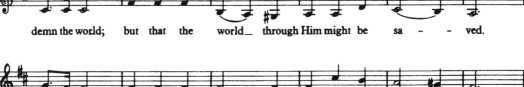

demn the world; but that the world through Him might be sa - - - ved.

demn the world; but that the world_ through Him might be sa - - - ved.

demn the world; but that the world_ through Him might be sa - - - ved.

41

10 Litany of the Passion

To be sung by the Choir and Congregation

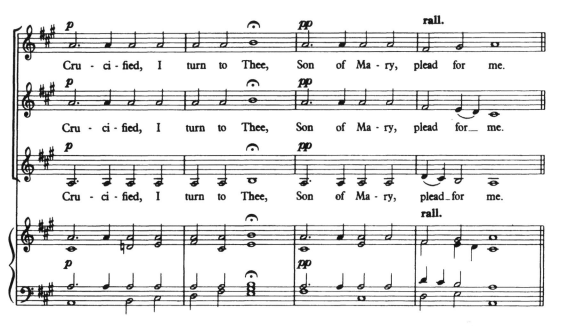

By the treachery and trial,
  By the blows and sore distress,
By desertion and denial,
  By Thine awful loneliness:
    Crucified, I turn to Thee,
    Son of Mary, plead for me.

By Thy look so sweet and lowly,
  While they smote Thee on the Face,
By Thy patience, calm and holy,
  In the midst of keen disgrace:
    Crucified, I turn to Thee,
    Son of Mary, plead for me.

By the hour of condemnation,
  By the blood which trickled down,
When, for us and our salvation,
  Thou didst wear the robe and crown:
    Crucified, I turn to Thee,
    Son of Mary, plead for me.

By the path of sorrows dreary,
  By the Cross, Thy dreadful load,
By the pain, when, faint and weary,
  Thou didst sink upon the road:
    Crucified, I turn to Thee,
    Son of Mary, plead for me.

By the Spir-it which could ren-der Love for hate and good for ill,

By the mer-cy, sweet and ten-der, Poured up-on Thy mur-derers still:

Cru-ci-fied, I turn to Thee, Son of Ma-ry, plead for me.

11 Jesus said, 'Father, forgive them'

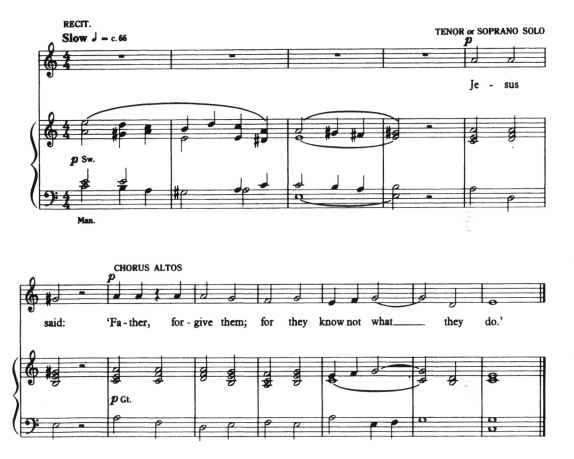

12 So Thou liftest Thy divine petition

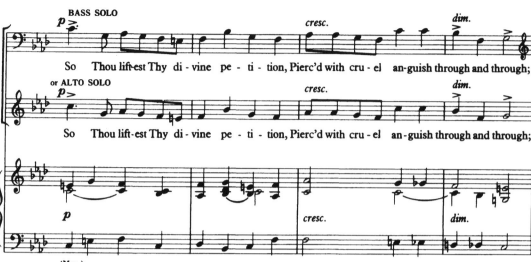

BASS SOLO

So Thou lift-est Thy di-vine pe-ti-tion, Pierc'd with cru-el an-guish through and through;

or ALTO SOLO

So Thou lift-est Thy di-vine pe-ti-tion, Pierc'd with cru-el an-guish through and through;

(Man.)

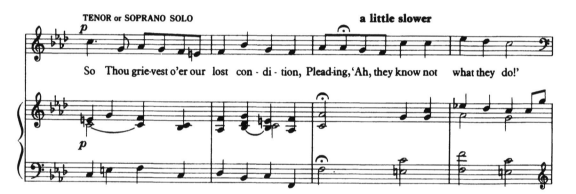

TENOR or SOPRANO SOLO

a little slower

So Thou grie-vest o'er our lost con-di-tion, Plead-ing, 'Ah, they know not what they do!'

rall.

BASS SOLO
pp with expression

Oh! 'twas love,

or ALTO SOLO
pp with expression

Oh! 'twas love,

rall.

dim.

48

So Thou plead-est, Yea, he knew not, yea, he knew not-for

My sake, for-give, for My sake, for-give, for - give, for - give.

13 The Mystery of intercession

To be sung by the Choir and Congregation

Page 53 sheet music.

Final.

Yet, in the midst of the tor-ture and shame, Je-sus, the Cru-ci-fied, breathes my name!

Won-der of won-ders, oh! how can it be? Je-sus, the Cru-ci-fied, pleads for me!

Lord, I have left Thee, I have denied,
Followed the world in my selfish pride;
Lord, I have joined in the hateful cry,
Slay Him, away with Him, crucify!
Lord, I have done it, oh! ask me not how;
Woven the thorns for Thy tortured Brow:
Yet in His pity so boundless and free,
Jesus, the Crucified, pleads for me!

Though thou hast left Me and wandered away,
Chosen the darkness instead of the day;
Though thou art covered with many a stain,
Though thou hast wounded Me oft and again:
Though thou hast followed thy wayward will;
Yet, in My pity, I love thee still.
Wonder of wonders it ever must be!
Jesus, the Crucified, pleads for me!

Jesus is dying, in agony sore,
Jesus is suffering more and more,
Jesus is bowed with the weight of His woe,
Jesus is faint with each bitter throe.
Jesus is bearing it all in my stead,
Pity Incarnate for me has bled;
Wonder of wonders it ever must be!
Jesus, the Crucified, pleads for me!

54

14 And one of his malefactors

★ Editorially suggested

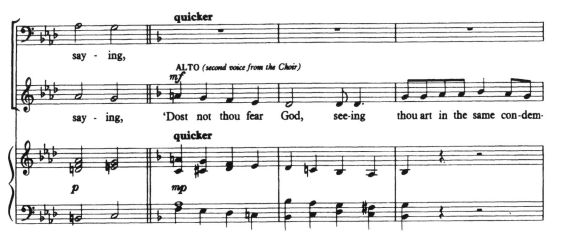

quicker

say - ing,

ALTO (second voice from the Choir)

say - ing, 'Dost not thou fear God, see-ing thou art in the same con-dem-

quicker

na - tion? And we in - deed just - ly; for we re - ceive the due re -

rall.

And he
or ALTO SOLO

ward of our deeds: but this man hath done no - thing a - miss.' And he

rall.

15 The adoration of the crucified

To be sung by the Choir and Congregation

vine, yet still di - vin - est In Thy dy - ing love for man.

vine, yet still di - vin - est In Thy dy - ing love for man.

vine, yet still di - vin - est In Thy dy - ing love for man.

I a - dore Thee, I a - dore Thee! Thank - ful at Thy feet to
I a - dore Thee, I a - dore Thee! Born of wo - man yet Di -

I a - dore Thee, I a - dore Thee! Thank - ful at Thy feet to
I a - dore Thee, I a - dore Thee! Born of wo - man yet Di -

I a - dore Thee, I a - dore Thee! Thank - ful at Thy feet to
I a - dore Thee, I a - dore Thee! Born of wo - man yet Di -

be;
vine: Stained with sins I kneel be - fore Thee, Sweet - est

I have heard Thy ac - cent thrill - ing, Lo! I

come, for Thou art will - ing Me to par - don, ev - en me.
Je - su, I im - plore Thee Make me ev - er on - ly Thine.

16 When Jesus therefore saw his mother

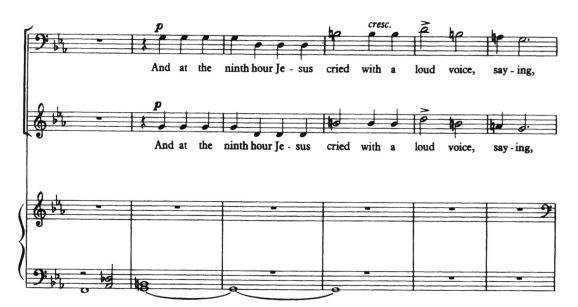

And at the ninth hour Je - sus cried with a loud voice, say - ing,

And at the ninth hour Je - sus cried with a loud voice, say - ing,

FULL
S I

adagio

'My God, My God, why hast Thou for - sa - ken Me?'

S II

'My God, My God, why hast Thou for - sa - ken Me?'

A

'My God, My God, why hast Thou for - sa - ken Me?'

adagio

17 Is it nothing to you?

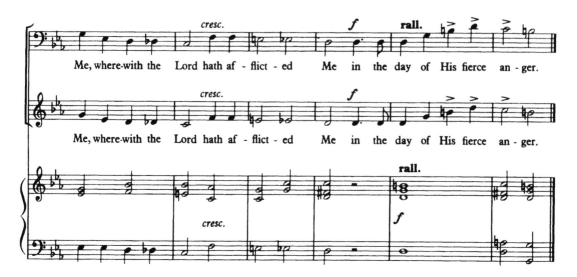

Me, where-with the Lord hath af - flict - ed Me in the day of His fierce an - ger.

Me, where-with the Lord hath af - flict - ed Me in the day of His fierce an - ger.

18 The appeal of the crucified

From the Throne of His Cross, the

From the Throne of His Cross, the

From the Throne of His Cross, the

ye that pass by? I laid My e-ter-nal power a-side, I came from the

Home of the Glo-ri-fied, A babe, in the low-ly cave to

lie; Is it no-thing to you, all ye that pass by?

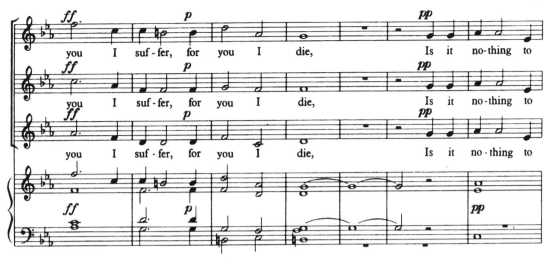

you I suf-fer, for you I die, Is it no-thing to

you, all ye that pass by? Oh!

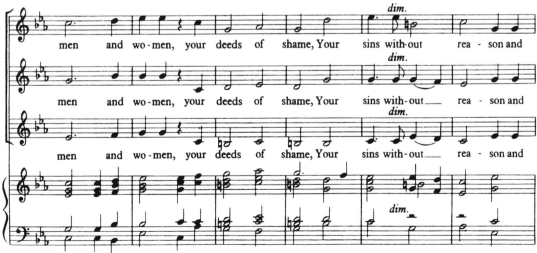

men and wo-men, your deeds of shame, Your sins with-out rea-son and

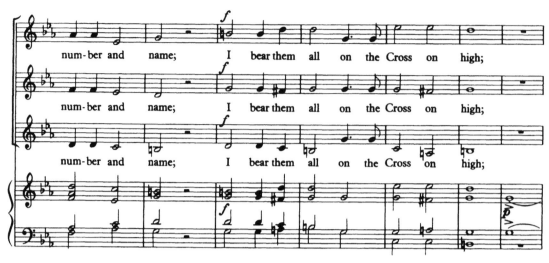

num-ber and name; I bear them all on the Cross on high;

Is it no-thing to you? Is it no-thing to you that I

bow My Head? And no-thing to you that My Blood is shed? O

per-ish-ing souls to you I cry, Is it no-thing to you?

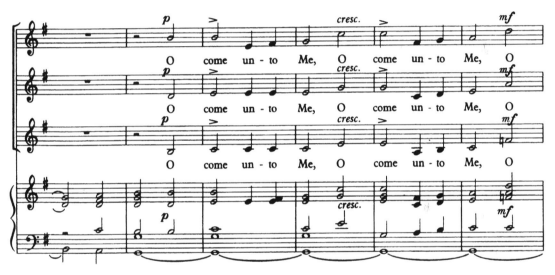

O come un-to Me, O come un-to Me, O

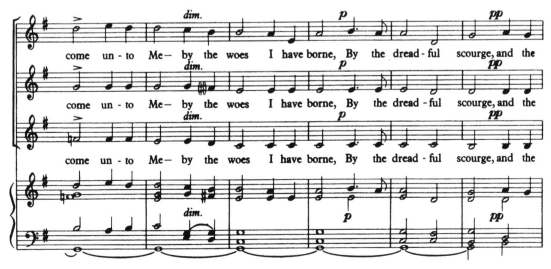

come un-to Me— by the woes I have borne, By the dread-ful scourge, and the

crown of thorns, By these, I im-plore you to hear My cry, Is it

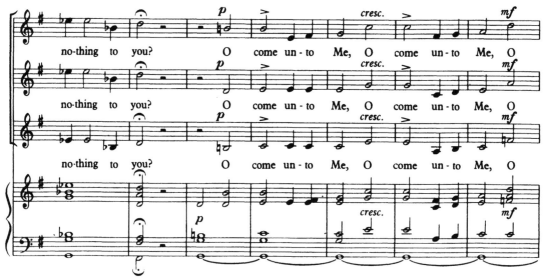

no-thing to you? O come un-to Me, O come un-to Me, O

come un-to Me— this aw-ful price, Re-demp-tion's tre-men-dous

sac - ri - fice— Is paid for you, is paid for you— Oh,

sac - ri - fice— Is paid for you, is paid for you— Oh,

sac - ri - fice— Is paid for you, is paid for you—, Oh,

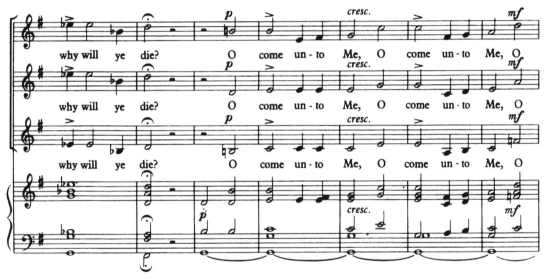

why will ye die? O come un - to Me, O come un - to Me, O,

why will ye die? O come un - to Me, O come un - to Me, O

why will ye die? O come un - to Me, O come un - to Me, O

come un - to Me— For why will ye die, for why will ye die? O

come un - to Me— For why will ye die, for why will ye die? O

come un - to Me— For why will ye die, for why will ye die? O

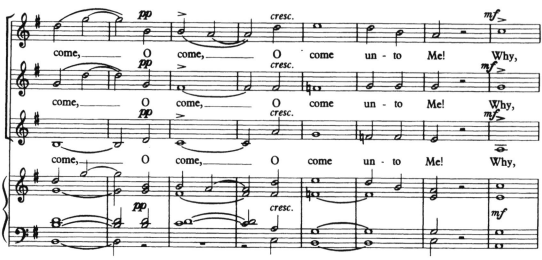

come,_____ O come,_____ O come un-to Me! Why,

come,_____ O come,_____ O come un-to Me! Why,

come,_____ O come,_____ O come un-to Me! Why,

come,_____ O come,_____ O come un-to Me! Why,

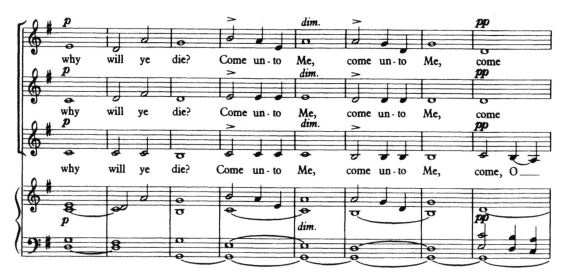

why will ye die? Come un-to Me, come un-to Me, come

why will ye die? Come un-to Me, come un-to Me, come

why will ye die? Come un-to Me, come un-to Me, come, O_____

to Me.

to Me.

come un-to Me.

Man.

19 After this, Jesus knowing that all things were now accomplished

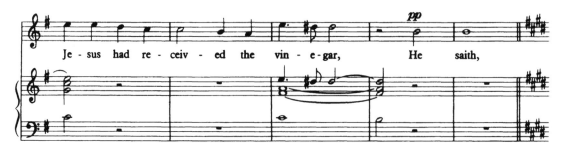

Je - sus had re - ceiv - ed the vin - e - gar, He saith,

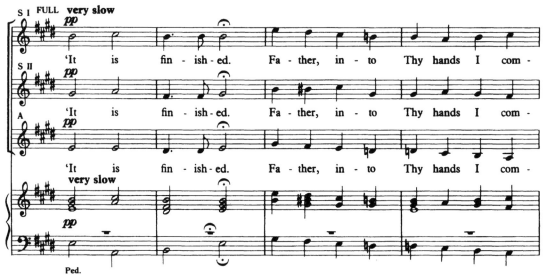

S I **FULL** **very slow**
'It is fin - ish - ed. Fa - ther, in - to Thy hands I com -

S II
'It is fin - ish - ed. Fa - ther, in - to Thy hands I com -

A
'It is fin - ish - ed. Fa - ther, in - to Thy hands I com -

very slow

Ped.

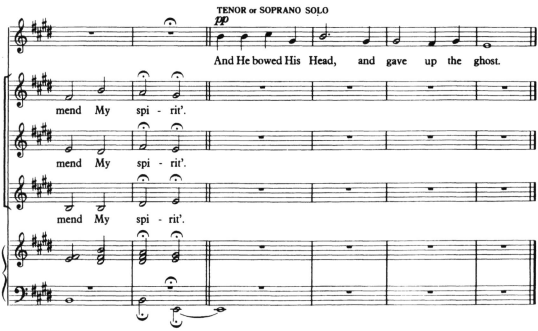

TENOR or SOPRANO SOLO
And He bowed His Head, and gave up the ghost.

mend My spi - rit'.

mend My spi - rit'.

mend My spi - rit'.

20 For the love of Jesus

To be sung by the Choir and Congregation

All for Jesus—Thou wilt give us
  Strength to serve Thee, hour by hour;
None can move us from Thy presence,
  While we trust Thy love and power.

All for Jesus—at Thine altar
  Thou wilt give us sweet content;
There, dear Lord, we shall receive Thee
  In the solemn Sacrament.

All for Jesus—Thou hast loved us;
  All for Jesus—Thou hast died;
All for Jesus—Thou art with us;
  All for Jesus Crucified.

All for Jesus—all for Jesus—
  This the Church's song must be;
Till, at last, her sons are gathered
  One in love and one in Thee.

Novello & Company Limited

Choral Music for Female and Boys' Voices

Bach: Ten Chorales arranged by César Geoffray for SSA

Carey Blyton: Ladies Only five songs for unaccompanied SSA

Brahms: Songs of Love arranged for SSA & piano. Piano duet accompaniment
        on sale.

Coleridge-Taylor: Hiawatha's Wedding Feast arranged for SSAA & piano.

Fauré: Messe Basse & Other Sacred Works arranged by *Desmond Ratcliffe*
        for SSA & piano or organ.

Fauré: Requiem arranged by *Desmond Ratcliffe* for SBar (or SA) soli, SSA
        chorus & orchestra.

Holst: Seven Part-Songs for SSA & strings

Michael Hurd: Charms & Ceremonies for unison voices, S(S)A & piano or
        string orchestra.
        Flower Songs for S(S)A & string orchestra or piano.
        Missa Brevis for SSA & organ or piano or string orchestra.

Pergolesi: Stabat Mater for SA soli, SA chorus & orchestra.

John Philips: Eight Negro Spirituals arranged for unaccompanied SSA.

Purcell: Come Ye Sons of Art arranged by Maurice Blower for SSA & piano or
        strings.

Aulis Sallinen: Song Around A Song for unaccompanied children's chorus (SSA)

Stainer: Crucifixion arranged by Desmond Ratcliffe for TB (or SA) soli, SSA
        chorus & organ.

Vivaldi: Gloria arranged by Desmond Ratcliffe for SSA, trumpet in C, oboe, strings
        & organ.